YO-BEK-089

Rhythm & Muse

Shades of Thought in Cadence and Voices Within

Poetry with Prose
by Thomas MacCalla

*To Scott
the one & two
great lovers
Thomas MacCalla*

KP

KIN PRODUCTIONS

KIN PRODUCTIONS

Copyright © 2007 by Thomas MacCalla. All rights reserved
Published by Kin Productions
7910 Ivanhoe Avenue, La Jolla, CA 92037
www.kinproductions.com
Printed in the United States of America. First Edition.

No part of this multimedia publication may be reproduced,
stored in a retrieval system, or transmitted, in any form
or by any means, without the prior permission in writing
from the publisher or as expressly permitted by law.

Library of Congress Cataloging-in-Publication Data available.

ISBN:1-933556-65-X

ISBN:978-1-933556-65-9

Cover Design by Jon Walker.
Photographs by Thomas MacCalla and Courtesy Contributors

Dedicated to:

Jacque Caesar, my wife,
mother of our four children
and my best friend.

Table of Contents

Rhythm & Muse

Prelude

Part 1, Shades of Thought in Cadence

Sepiatones

Somewhere I heard a writer paint a song; Sepiatones, Sepia Saga; Explaining Me; You and Me; Eventually I Came Out of Darkness; Mirror Image

Color of Life at Home

Inside the little room that felt large; House on the Hill; Parent's Legacy; Welcome to the Way Station; Evans of the World; The Glass Chess Set; Siblings; Satin Doll; Counterpoint (Chorus Lines from "Love Joy"); Mother's Day; Tribute to JC; Rx; Lyrics from "I wanted you to know"; Love Is; Let's Grow Our Love; Healing Hearts; Lifetime Eclipse; Thanksgiving Moment; The Measure of Self

Footnote: "The Gift from God"; Lyrics from "I've got to be strong"

Wordscapes

Wordscapes; El Centro West; Brown Prism; Framing a Lazy Day; Window Sighting; Vista del Mar; By the Ocean's Side; Voyager's Mirror of the Sea; Rocky Mountaineer Rail Tour; Winter's Advent; Grand Canyon Rim; Tahoe Blue

Interlude

"Endless Beginnings"; "As I was saying"

*Expressions of wonder, sketches of life
wrapped in word whispers, poetic passion,
thought and reflections colored in pastels,
voices within harmonizing blue notes.
Welcome to the message and the music.*

Prelude

The turn of the new century marked many new beginnings. One of them was a series of life reflections that I crafted in cadence and called Sepiatones. That unfinished work offered personal sounds painted in shades of brown and tints of blue. It represented a deep-seeded desire to sketch a silent me, wrapped in rhythmic expression. The thrust was a celebration of indelible images spawned by the love of family, friendship, and the sense of people-hood. I now want to finalize those thoughts and feelings, share the joy, and set quiet moments free with echoes of wonderment put to a self-styled beat and universal chords.

Continuing to wrestle with the gnawing presence of uncertainty and our curiosity about tomorrow, I decided to amplify the voices resonating within and pen word orchestrations begging for release. The reconstruction of a seasoned life began to unfold, starting in the middle of timeless tales of "before" and the endless quest for a hereafter. It grew larger and louder with questions about the accuracy of the past, the assumptions of custom, the thin line between purpose in life and the possibility of an eternal void. The realization was a better understanding of love, dreams, and relationships woven with words.

Welcome, then, to *Rhythm and Muse*, a different kind of book. It is a testimony to life wrapped in color and subliminal sounds. The goal is to create a stylistic prose that weaves verse, visual art, and the pulse of music into a multimedia statement. Some of the reflections and images are laced with photo art and water colors, while others dance to the original lyrics of kin. The sum is the song of a person born into an arbitrary, social cage with the door ajar, a human being able to recall pathways to everywhere, thinking holistically and smiling with determination to be free.

Music of the Mind

Rhythm and Muse is words put to music,
playing life's everyday tunes in off-white,
crafted in shades of thought and emotions,
remixed with refrains of beige reflections.

Follow the movements of warmth, dark, and hope,
in the cadence of measured syllables,
laced with the soft sounds of voices within
balancing the simple and the complex.

Listen to a repaired heart sing aloud,
testifying to the meaning of life,
phrasing sentiments with insightful notes,
while leaving room for interpretation.

Write Reasoning

Brilliant lights awake a sleeping poet –
dormant stirrings come alive in soft sounds,
blending thoughts and feelings in verse and prose
to revisit the past and make it whole.

Faint school lessons become insightful hooks –
discounted deeds gain new life and meaning,
empowering the self with a latent force
to counter blind acceptance with vision.

Coleridge wrote romantic fantasies –
idyllic tales and poetic folklore
preserving the spirit of yesteryear
for escape into tomorrow's new world.

Creative minds are daylight star gazers –
curious souls exploring the unknown,
searching inner secrets of outer worlds
so discovery can alter thinking.

Notice the ripple of first pebbles tossed –
West and East wisdom begin to converge,
seeding common ground for sharing knowledge
to enlighten and respect difference.

Courtesy of Shirley Livingston

Part 1, Shades of Thought in Cadence

Somewhere I heard a writer paint a song.
I imitated out of ignorance,
only to learn that I, too, could sing words
and color the melodic script in me.
So, I sing soulful portraits in cadence,
Sepiatone moods and thoughts about being.

Sepiatones is a life's journey of word portraits in song seen through a brown prism. The adventure probes the hidden pathways of a healing heart and a curious mind. The unveiling was delayed for many years, but the will to write about the maze was stirred in earnest late in life. The new-found drive enabled me to fulfill a deep-seeded desire to relive defining choices and speculate on the side roads and those not taken. The trek began with a private piece called *Sepiatones*, shades of thought penned with a rhythmic beat. It explored the depths of personal space and put pluralism into perspective against the backdrop of the dominant culture.

Having discovered the writer's discipline at dusk, I was ready to recount the memorable growing-up years and dismiss the hurt of ignorance as the way of the world. What follows is a sepia excursion that reflects the light and dark tones of a young man riding life's circuit. As such, you are invited to witness a presumptuous poet recreate the sensitivity of the inner eye and paint pastel images on Nature's window. Note the chorus lines and refrains of songs that speak of the righteousness, callousness, curiosity, and creativity that come in many human colors. Hopefully, you will enjoy the performance and the gallery.

Sepia Saga

Born sepia, unaware of what lies ahead,
a lifelong run with an uncertain finish line.
Grew freely and curious about the unknown,
constantly reacting to arbitrary rules.
Still growing, challenging prevailing ignorance,
a popular game that flaunts order and breeds war.
Pray on occasion, wondering who knows the Truth.
when everyone lays claim to Divine Mystery.
Die sepia, leaving today for tomorrow,
hoping the promise of afterward is revealed.

Explaining Me

I was born a long time ago, yet I still feel young and alive. I was educated formally by parish nuns and the Jesuits, but informally and indelibly at home by my two older and talented brothers, two even older and talented sisters, and two enterprising and supportive parents, Esther and Reuben, also known as Lady Esther and Doc. They were soul mates for over sixty years and raised two older Jamaican-born daughters and three American-born sons to take their place in the world.

The Lady and Doc reigned over the legendary 896 Stratford Avenue in Bridgeport, Connecticut, the one-time industrial capital of New England. They ruled from a room at the top of the stairs in a turn-of the century structure that was anchored in a neighborhood of third and fourth generation personalities living in worn, vintage houses and mixed-use storefronts. Doc was the reserved thinker and "proper sport" who spoke with a recognizable Caribbean accent. Esther was the enterprising homemaker and subtle mastermind with an uptown flair. She used her charm and wit to survive and transform a neighborhood landmark dwelling into shared, living-working quarters for an immediate and extended family.

The sixteen-room, brown colored, clapboard building had a huge basement and housed oversized living and dining room spaces on the first floor. Across the wide hall, which doubled as a waiting room, was a dental office and lab. At the end of the hall was a spiral staircase that led to a second-floor with five bedrooms, a dressmaker's room, a bathroom, a third floor door that led to a large attic with a spare bedroom and an open area with high rafters that doubled as a playground sprinkled with clutter.

The three-storied home had lots of yard space with two garages and a huge rear barn that stored Mr. Hoffman's Barnum and Bailey circus equipment until the annual show came to town. The big house with the dentist inside was flanked by other multiple-storied houses fronting trolley-tracks on a main road, which was noticeably marred by winter potholes and bordered by worn, sorted store-fronts and immigrant households steeped in ethnic pride. Personal contact was commonplace, all of which started with children at play. Neighborly doors opened slowly, feeding budding relationships with the frequency of folk exchange. Over time, the trolleys gave way to the local bus line and an economic downturn changed the character of the environment. Eventually, the spent hamlet was declared a nuisance, obstructing the path of progress. Through the power of eminent domain the street gave way to the Connecticut Turnpike.

During my growing up years, I cherished the advice of my brothers, Eric and Alfred, and the nurturing love of my sisters, Hazel and Ruby. Although I was neither the talented artist, nor the mechanical wizard that my brothers were, I knew that I had something special to offer. Age separated us by ten and six years respectively. The time span between me and my sisters stretched into the twenties. I was ever-curious, ready to dabble into everything. I can still hear the drone of my mother's words "Do your thing son and don't let anyone try to stop you." I went to Prep school, college, and dutifully to Korea, fortunate enough to return home safely, ready to ride the higher learning circuit and fight the war on ignorance.

By 1940s standards, we were middle-class and Negro. Pride and perseverance to win the prize of being singled out for success captivated our being. We were self-empowered by the constant social struggle and motivated by the Negro network to blunt the prevailing ignorance and hurdle the racial divide. Mother was a "Girl Friend," a club member with Washingtonian breeding who skirted the fringes of Franklin's Black Bourgeoisie. She was the "Link" who operated a dress-making and slip-cover business at home. Father was one of the Jamaican sharp minds drawn from the Island, who, after graduating from a fledgling Howard University, crossed the color line of separate medical worlds and proudly opened his dental practice in the Nutmeg State.

As the family's youngest treasure, I was the beneficiary of love and encouragement and "spoiled for my own good." I was mentored by siblings, an assortment of relatives, new family members who lived in the house from time-to-time, and by occasional boarders who filled the other rooms to help pay the mortgage and the lights.

The music beat of the fifties, sixties and seventies paced a joyful ride of fun and toil that made the battle "to overcome" tolerable. Although being "the first" was still prideful, the newness of the heralded badge lost its luster. Other battles had to be won, and I wanted to join the fray from my generation's vantage point. I accepted change as the constant companion of growth. The by-product of this reality was reflected in the receptive and competitive spirit of my children who had to make new friends in school on a regular basis. I fed the urge to know more. I went to UCLA, walked the city streets, worked for money, and traveled abroad to enlarge my knowledge and experience. In the process I became a community practitioner, citizen journalist, and lifelong learner.

Having reflected on the travesty of getting ahead at all cost, I recognized that it was self-imposed slavery. Success was not to be measured by personal accomplishment and accolades, but by self-reflection and communion with family and friends. In this shining light, words took on a new meaning. My interest in writing grew by fusing poetic thought with daily talk and lessons learned by teaching school. I dabbled in journalism, toyed with the abstract, and wrote to myself while pursuing a second career in higher education. This freedom to be and desire to share mirror images of a lifespan served me well.

Today, I am "Black, Sepia, Whole and Wiser," incorporating the beauty of the human family wrestling with tradition and ignoring issues of turf. I decided to release my writing-urge into the open in a creative way. The images and insights of my thoughts and feelings were beginning to surface. I rediscovered some of my younger private notes in verse and countered procrastination with a new confidence. After facing the ghost of reaching forty and passing the mid century mark, the consciousness of age became grist and forced me to focus on what is important.

At sixty I began to write in earnest. Although the style and rhythmic beats were in a formative stage, the drive was ingrained. The free-fall of ensuing years that I penned in *Sepiatones* reflected a form and style that continued to mature. When seventy-five arrived, I was ready to commit to print and the virtual world so that I could release a free spirit that would connect everything with everything else. I wanted to find meaning in new combinations of the old, discover sameness in dissimilarities and appreciate the pace and paradox of life.

You and Me

You, like me, are born in complete innocence,
finding our identity early in life,
fearing how, and how hard the last door will shut.

We all center on the *me* who lives inside,
harboring wonderment and uncertainty,
chasing confusion, feeding the love of self.

We are what we know, feel, believe, and ignore,
marveling at others in a crowded world,
enamored by the lure of peace and freedom.

You, like me, were bred with inherited truths,
listening to dissonant cultural sounds
without appreciating our common bond.

We seek wisdom, despise abuse of power,
protest ignorant voices that lead to war
and evil deeds that compromise truth and love.

We both can shape a promising future
if you and I are willing to share ourselves
and respect difference in people and thought.

Eventually I Came Out of Darkness

Eventually I came out of darkness-
beginning years lost and found through questions.
I lived in the blind for more than twelve years,
thirteen, if you count my sleep with mother.
I peered through darkness at an early age,
testing teen years on taunting ethnic streets.

I looked up to my family heroes,
I teased trouble short of embarrassment,
saved by sports, music and Jesuit hands.
I landed in a dark place steeped in war,
opened windows to freedom and to fun,
guided by angels and a love waiting.

I returned to a place torn by distrust,
divided by ignorance, filled with hope.
I charted a path of independence,
sharpening many unanswered questions.
I became adventurer, street scholar,
trying to fathom new urban discord.

I questioned the motives of righteousness,
championing our interdependence.
I learned new skills in the ivory halls,
wondering how wisdom missed the mark.
I stayed in free-fall until earth drew near,
seventy plus years, and out of darkness.

Mirror Image

Who do you see in the mirror?
Take a deep breath – look at yourself,
unscrew the complicated head,
strip the selfish coating inside,
come blink at fantasy with me,
cross the bridge over River Love,
enjoy the moment; now return,
relax in knowing who you are.
Listen to the whispers inside
and you will learn more about you.

Color of Life at Home

We all have family albums that recall our growing up years and bonds with friends and relatives. Hopefully, you can relate to some of the sentiments and smiles expressed in this coloring of life at home and snapshots of family fun, pride, and togetherness.

Inside the little room that felt large…

Jesting and storytelling are memorable remnants of younger days that follow children into adulthood. For me, telling tales and stringing spontaneous thoughts together was almost second nature. I was Dad, the friendly giant, master of bedtime stories. Mom was the giant's master, the beautiful wise one and keeper of secrets.

It started inside the little room that felt large, a front-corner bedroom where I planted seeds at nighttime, watered the fertile field of impressionable minds, stretched reality and mixed the ordinary with mysterious and humorous yarns to make the serious indelible. I played word games and sketched silliness on an imaginary canvas. I made mental maps with inviting signposts and a curious path to follow. I modeled the way of words and painted images with wild ideas to nourish a passion for creativity and feed dreams. Eventually, the seeds would take root and become the grist for make-believe.

There they sat – two siblings perched on a tattered shag carpet awaiting the nightly "lights out" refrain. They listened intently as an animated father-figure read aloud from an invisible script. With a devilish smile he would recount a day's routine that may or may not have happened. Comfortably grounded, a wide-eyed son and a dutiful daughter listened to magical journeys in a re-arranged world. Smiling eyes reveled in awe, storing jewels of fun and fantasy that they could keep forever.

Tomorrow would arrive suddenly. By the next new day they would get their chance to create stories and read aloud to their young and other little captive audiences. That room would always feel large.

House on the Hill

From 1948 to 6251, numbers of places on non-descript streets, we grew as individuals and as one together. A house is more than a shelter. A house is a marker of indelible moments where family falls in love with itself. It is the recycled fertile ground that yields a fresh kinship tree with branches of soft steel and creative leaves. Our house on the hill at 6251 was the spot where togetherness was cradled. The color of our house was the color inside.

Sixty two fifty one, a place called home,
a symbol of life with freedom to be.
Sibling tales and music took center stage,
humming hope that parents live forever.

Sixty two fifty one, a gamble lost,
a legacy rekindled down the road.
Adults reunited through family,
knowing that we all live on borrowed time.

Parent's Legacy

We are our parents now.
Time has made us older
and as wise as they were.

We are the new elders,
preserving yesterday,
beacons for tomorrow.

Our children become us.
Time will make them older
and wiser than we are.

They inherit the past,
replaying lessons learned,
creating the future.

Long live the legacy,
nurturing shared values,
personifying love.

Welcome to the Way Station

It has been a long time coming, and no one could stop it.
Your first three hundred sixty five days marks the beginning
of the never-ending road that leads somewhere and nowhere.
Thank you for sharing your new life with those under your spell.

This day comes once a year with many salutes to follow.
More three hundred sixty five days will brighten the countdown
to enjoyment, fulfillment, and your legacy of love.
Thank you for your innocence and becoming who you are.

Evans of the World

The future is not about us who contemplate it.
Tomorrow's time belongs to the Evan's of the world,
the third generation of his, her and their offspring,
obliging authority and aware of themselves,
soaking up newness and creating different moods,
singing new old tunes until they're caught in future think.

What's behind the colors and shapes of finger painting?
What triggers child's play and video game maneuvers?
What coaxes clever thoughts and the surprising use of words?
Why does fun suddenly turn sad in a happy room?
Why is silence so frightening and saving senseless?
Why are some things important, yet never stay the same?

These are the hallmarks of an Evan's world fast forward.
Tomorrow's time awaits new players and reshaped rules,
a global generation thinking about their turn,
simulating problems, crossing cultural borders,
freely communicating while bridging time and space
to rewrite destiny's script for the Evan's in line.

The Glass Chess Set

It started with chess games to teach my son logic
to explore pathways of thinking and consequence,
transmitting the desire to learn and create,
despite the time it would take for the child to win.

First-born's early years, filled with fun and fantasy,
flashing mental prowess couched in buffoonery,
foreshadowing dim signals of male dominance,
were blessed with compassion and sense of family.

It continued with lessons to be one's person,
while growing with my mate to be the guardians,
charting the nurturing course that we envisioned,
knowing we are our parents now, transparent pawns.

Off-spring multiplied between four year intervals,
spacing sibling sisters and a baby brother,
framing special worlds underneath their own bright stars,
until music's meteor brought them together.

Now, they are in line to write tomorrow's lyrics,
blending the artistry of family and friends,
with extended love and camaraderie's treasure,
creating the joy of living and shared success.

Siblings

Siblings write separate diaries in deeds
to create their own living masterpiece.

Eldest namesake steeped in integrity,
defines himself in focused fashion,
sharing self in uncompromising ways,
building sandcastles that withstand attack,
parceling summer seeds from Leo's lair,
extending the spirit of family.

Masterful lady healer, next in line,
self-styled artist of anticipation,
seasoned by wisdom and persistent grace,
a caring mother and patient partner,
waiting to slay the aging mind's menace,
with medical marvel and sharing faith.

Sensitive sister, gifted performer,
born to live singing and improvising,
following her heart in a wonderland,
spreading warmth with quick wit and laughter,
showcasing friendship and generous soul,
hoping to realize sweet dreams deferred.

Younger brother, self-disciplined artist,
music maker talent with a keen ear,
crafting and coloring a new blend of sound,
silent sage dressed in unnoticed manhood,
allowed to define his space and be free,
harboring a heartbeat for someone true.

Siblings compose individual song
to celebrate their bond in harmony.

Satin Doll

Here's to my Love-a-bye-to Broadway.
Radiant redwood in her stage domain,
last of the autumn leaves and first at springtime.
Born to sing and dance to showcase her soul,
sharing joy and pain in triumphant love.

Stay satin and keep the North Star in sight.
Sail the seas of merriment and applause,
gracing halls with your laughter and friendship.
Sing sassy notes from your deep-pitted soul,
saving some of love's joy for dreams on hold.

Counterpoint
Chorus Lines from "Love Joy" by Sylvia MacCalla

You are my love, you are my joy. You bring me sunshine everyday, and
I want to thank you from the bottom of my heart for bringing me so much love,
so much joy, sunshine everyday and I want to thank you from the bottom of my heart.

You never lost your innocence. After all this time no jaded heart.
You live your life with an open mind so I look to you to guide me through,
lift me up, carry on, and bring the sunshine my way.

(Courtesy of Charlotte Caesar)

Mother's Day

Enjoy spring Lilacs and the Iris blooms
parading delicate charm and fragrance
on this May Day ordained for Mother Love.
Notice how they smile with fresh morning grace,
stretching yesterday into tomorrow.

Mother of Passion and Family Love
wrap the warmth of the moment for yourself,
living the dream in a world you've defined.
Savor the joy of remembrance and hope,
dressed in soft floral lavender and white.

Tribute to JC

You're the greatest source of love and support,
compassionate healer of broken hearts,
keen observer of human behavior,
and the best person to have as a friend.

You're the honest listener of silent pain,
maternal wizard of infant music,
learned doctor of family discord,
the best person to have as a conscience.

You're a kind and selfless human spirit,
unassuming companion in a crowd,
master of compromise and circumstance,
the best person to have as a mentor.

You're a hero of the daily struggle
champion and a personal treasure,
unheralded wisdom beyond belief,
the best person to be with forever.

Rx

The heart throbs for love and life
soon to fade as memories.
Seize the moment from time's grip,
salvaging wishes on hold.
Savor and share life's bounty,
scored in music of the soul.

I Wanted You to Know

Lyrics by Reuben and Sylvia Mac Calla (CD)

There comes a time in your life when you wonder why you're here on this earth -
You don't know.
Suddenly it's all so clear. You were the one to show me the way.
You gave me strength and give me love that means so much to me.
I wanted you to know.

You are the sun that shines in me a feeling of love that sets me free-
in my life.
You're all that I ever needed in my life (yah) and I hope that you will see.
That after some time has gone away deep in my heart you will stay.
You're all that I ever needed in my life -
and I wanted you to know.

I sit all alone with my thoughts and then suddenly you appear in my mind safe and sound. It's nice to know you're always there. When I'm down you set me high. You set me free so I can fly away, but then, you're always there to come back to. I wanted you to know.

You are the sun that shines in me a feeling of love that sets me free-
You're all that I ever wanted in my life and I hope that you will see.
After some time has gone away deep in my heart you will stay.
You're all that I ever needed in my life and I wanted you to know.

I know that this love will carry on (deep in my heart). Take a moment for yourself, so you'll stay strong. I hope that you know that you've provided me, undeniably, with the (love and the touch of your heart). It's good to know that you are always there.

You are the sun that shines in me, a feeling of love that sets me free.
You're all that I ever wanted in my life and I hope that you will see.
After some time has gone away deep in my heart that I know you will stay.

Deep in my heart I know that you will stay (shine in me, ooh my heart). You know I'll always love you and your with me each and everyday and with you here there's nothing to fear. I love you so, and I wanted you to know.

You are the sun that shines in me. You're shining on me, you bring me the sun. I love you so and I wanted you to know. You're more than the sun. Let me tell you again. You're shining on me, you bring me the sun. Love you so, and I wanted you to know.

"Mauve Roses" Courtesy of Ruth Richardson

Love Is

Love is an unconditional exchange of hearts,
committed to caring and growing memories.

Love is celebrating a life worth living,
humble servant, confidant, and healer of hurt.

Love is a grafting of souls in tune with each other,
a sensual symphony of togetherness.

Love is the silent song of wishful lives,
embarking on a journey of shared joy and pain.

Love is yielding to gain spiritual triumph,
a prayer for fertile seeds to leave a legacy.

Love is a willingness to go beyond oneself,
breeding compassion, forgiveness, and lasting hope.

Let's Grow Our Love

Why is the sun brighter somewhere else
and the moon is never quite so full?

Is there a somewhere without limits
filled with love and infinite beauty?

I wonder how we get there from here
when we compromise the possible,
shun the wisdom of simplicity,
the promise of imagination,
or the power of sharing ourselves.

What does it take to realize a dream
that we create in private moments?

Can we dance without the driving beat
and follow the rhythm of our hearts?

Let's grow our love and build a new world,
with meaning to the rest of our lives,
each willing to give along the way
respecting the spirit of the soul,
knowing we've reached our destination.

Healing Hearts

I would not be here today if I did not live so long.

The honor belongs to modern medicine,
coupled with my mate's uncanny sense of health,
mixed with the depths of enduring family love,
compassion of friendship and human spirit,
allowing me to see what is important.

I thank the Heavens for the reprieve and the renewal.

The ordeal of her heart's failure humbled me,
cushioned the jolt to my body's circuitry,
repaired by the healing blend of East and West,
vested in the quadrant of integration,
enabling me to discover simple truths.

Lifetime Eclipse

Fifty, Seventy, Seventy-Five–
indelible numbers converging
on a stretched string of calendar months
to celebrate a lifetime eclipse,
marking marriage and testifying
to enduring love and family,
sharing a joy to be remembered.

Fifty years from nineteen fifty four –
seventy years from first breathe of life,
seventy five years as Esther's last gift,
one hundred ninety five years as One.

Fifty, Seventy, Seventy Five–
mid-summer Moon crossing winter's Sun,
fading into memory's mirror
to reflect a full life worth living,
saluting love and togetherness
to recognize eternal friendship
enjoying tomorrow's dream today.

Thanksgiving Moment

Our endless journey starts in a conscious world,
framed by the void of before and after,
kept alive by family and memories.

Let us pay tribute on this day of thanks
to relish the bonds of kin and friendship,
and share the treasure of togetherness.

Honor the Font of Love and Source of Life
to restore faith through reflection and hope
amidst random fortune and suffering,

Celebrate this moment of thanksgiving,
paying homage in traditional form
extending ourselves to those near and far.

Return to tomorrow's uneven road,
wanting to spread the warmth of the respite
knowing that giving thanks humbles and frees.

The Measure of Self

How we treat one another
is a true measure of self,
knowing what is important
on an uncertain journey
filled with professions of faith.

Seeking answers in the dark
with a sense of honesty
is a game of sanity
protected by the promise
of salvation forever.

Accept human frailty
and hurts of indifference
in a land of paradox,
choosing to be one's person
standing up for what seems right.

Love lives through relationships
and dies with self deception,
enduring disappointments
and the wrath of righteousness
to be a witness for Truth.

Footnote:

The Gift from God
(by Reuben MacCalla)

Can you hear what is truly in your heart?
It is the sound of your calling in the world.
The answers are unclear and the path is treacherous.
The questions are undeniably clear.
Do I have what it takes to carry out my calling?
Am I where I want to be? Does this define who I am? Am I happy?
This list is filled with endless questions that only the heart can answer.
The acceptance of negatives is what makes it hard to hear what is truly in your heart.
The gifts that god has given you are there, but they don't define who you are.
How you choose to use those gifts is up to you.
What you leave behind on this earth is how you are defined in the end.

I've Got To Be Strong

Lyrics by Reuben MacCalla (CD)

I need the strength to carry on.
It's been so hard to be strong.
What must I do to make it through?
I'm calling to you God
and I know that you will be here with me.

I've got to be strong
(it's gonna get better)
I've got to keep holding on. I know. I know.
(it will be worth it you'll see)
I've got to be strong.
(you will be happy)
I've got to keep holding on. I know. I know. I know.
(just keep on pushin', movin')

I've got to be strong for another day.
It's crazy that life has to work this way.
It's been so hard for me to understand.
That things don't work out the way we plan.

Why do I feel this sadness and pain?
Why do I always have to be strong?
What must I do to make it through
what seems like a lifetime?
and I know that you will be here with me.

Lord give me the strength to love again.
When is this going to end.
I've got to be strong. I know.
Can you here what I'm saying.

(I've got to be strong)
It's gonna get better.
(I've got to keep holding on. I know. I know.)
It's gonna work out I know it.
(I've got to be strong)
I just have to believe.
(I've got to keep holding on. I know. I know. I know.)
Just wait and see
(I've got to be strong)
I just know that.
(I've got to keep holding on. I know. I know)
Some way . Some how.
(I've got to be strong)
All I know. I've got to keep moving on
'cuz I've got to be strong.

Keep moving on. Keep pushing on
I know some day that it's going to get better.
Keep moving on. Keep pushing on.
Hold on tight. Just wait and see.
Keep moving on. Keep pushing on
I know some day that it's going to get better.
Keep moving on. Keep pushing on.
Hold on tight. Just wait and see.

Slot Canyon Abstract

Wordscapes

Coloring words to express the sap of the soul is an art form and a musical composition of the mind's eye in phrases and statements laced with descriptors and a measured beat. The following word images and pastel renderings portray the warmth of Nature's gallery. We begin by traveling west at dawn along the roadway from a desert floor then through the weathered-stoned mountain passes, skirting over the dry high clusters of pines and down to the beckoning Pacific shore. We then look through a brown prism to glimpse the mood that accompanies the struggle for equality and mutual respect, followed by an array of natural vistas and a symphony of hues that inspire the joy of life.

El Centro West

Cross the sea-level valley floor at dawn's light
for a private showing of desert contrasts.
Suspend that scheduled routine and free a soul
caged by reason and responsibility.
Ride the asphalt's centerline while carefully
listening to the echoes from mountain contours
relay the stillness of rock chips and boulders
with an impressive display of nothingness.
Continue the winding road to higher ground
courting deceptive curves with silent caution
until the roadway opens to greet the sky
and dirt gorges are replaced by green vistas.
Chase the summit markers that preface decent,
leaving behind the sandy daybreak magic,
hastening the stretch west to urban landscapes
and journey's end to start again the same day.

Brown Prism

Transparent flashes
of life passing by
colorless sketches
of forgotten deeds,
image reflections
of lingering ghosts,
distorted vistas
of human travail
in sepiatones
casting forgiveness.

Angry heirs aware
of lost history
chronicling the past,
to resurrect truth,
purging ignorance
to kill the race giant
by acclamation
on the global field
and forge humankind
into one spirit.

Framing a Lazy Day

Peering over the train trestle
to catch the water world's rim
before sunset dries the image.

Brushing sonar sounds on canvas
to draw fading light rays to shore,
scoring dark sky-lined seascapes.

Watercolor rhythm driving
pastel chords phrased in off-blue,
creating abstract melodies.

Greet the Pacific's dawning night
before the returning tide sings
another lazing day's refrain..

A Window Sighting

Behold wet shades of blue, edged in puffed white.
Peer through my words and glimpse at dawn's parade.

The sun sprinkles light on a morning sea,
with its constant chant from ruffled waters,
celebrating nature's massive domain.
She seems to be moving around the world,
reminding us of endurance and hope,
returning with another gift of life.

Come visit me. I live close to that place.
Share daybreak's invitation to vistas.

Flowered greenbelts border dwelling spaces,
aligned shingled frames with crimped viewing holes
lord over the roadway that crests the shore.
Waking moments capture the quiet storm
above rooftops of uniform quarters,
yielding to the daily buzz quelled at dusk..

Vista del Mar

Watch the ritual of white ruffled waves
approach land's end with relentless rhythm,
retreating after its brute course is spent.
Hear sounds of water fury resonate
from once blue panorama now turned steel,
giving notice the onslaught will return.

Drink the beauty of the hazy morning
whose airy shadow dulls the coastal force,
promising azure calm after clearing.
Give thanks for this free moment of respite
before the drone of daily life intrudes,
marring dawn's image of power and peace.

(Courtesy of Mary Helmreich)

By the Ocean's Side

Listen to the quiet intrigue of the open sea beckon.

Overwhelming vastness and sounds of tidewater pageantry
mesmerize and invite imagination to roam freely
and appreciate beauty, the power of simplicity.

Phantom sea herds faintly murmur in the watery distance,
blowing ashore the salt air vapor that cloaks the ocean's might
until rippling waves are spent and spread on a sandy carpet.

Black wet suits and a lone fly rod caster accent the vista,
sharing adventure lifestyles and the warmth of morning's glory
without disturbing the peacefulness of the panorama.

Talk to yourself and savor this moment by the ocean's side.

Voyager's Mirror of the Sea

You can't go there when everywhere is here.
Hearts cross, colors blend on a promenade,
connecting dots on a watery world.

Witness the generation jubilee.
Tongues babble, spirits share in harmony,
circling the inner and outer spaces.

See surreal glamour gloss over the week.
Costumes parade on cordoned indoor streets,
painting hues of fantasy and comfort.

Look through the cruise ship's horizon mirror.
Skies whisper, waves dance on changing seascapes,
casting the lure of beauty and balance.

Let the sounds of summer last forever.
Friends multiply, families bond anew,
exposing the myth of returning home.

Rocky Mountaineer Rail Tour

With heightened anticipation we pulled away from the Vancouver station yard, ready to capture the heralded Canadian Rocky Mountaineer Rail-tour of a lifetime. We started our journey as insightful observers and photography novices. I panned the wide outdoors with undisciplined motion, shooting everything in sight for the first one hundred kilometers with this magical digital device. Suddenly, the camera's red warning light flashed and triggered a frozen blank sensation inside. An instant rush of gloom struck and then stopped abruptly. The uneasy feeling was replaced by the wishful thought that the colorful eye of words could paint the scenes. What follows are some of those "visual clicks" translating the imagery of the photo lens into the personal impressions courting the first and last legs of the tour.

First Leg

City eyes marvel at Nature's canvas.
Trains traverse the Canadian Rockies.
Cross the Great Fraser and Thompson Canyon.
Murky brown and steel blue rivers converge.
Rails and roads track winding waterways.
Traces of worn warning posts dot the route.
Tree-studded cliffs caress unstable ground.
Wildlife roam ragged hills and valley floors.
Osprey perched on dead limbs survey lost land.
Aroma sage and rabbit weed flourish.
Root blossoms grace First Nation settlements.
Black Canyon reveals volcanic shadows.
Eroded rock formations boast beauty.
Tram cables slice the void of Hell's Gate Gorge.
High deserts overtake armies of trees.
Lunarscape tones cast spiritual auras.
Sunshine blasts accent white puffs and grim clouds.
Leave the Thompson and approach Kamloops Lake,
awaiting the lure of more dome sightings.

Last Leg

Record for memory the panorama.
Blue Sky impressions from Jasper to Banff.
Savor Nature's animated murals.
Snow-capped mountain peaks lord over vastness.
Ice fields and avalanche shoots dress the land.
Twisted canyons, meandering rapids.
Glacial lakes, powder spills, and waterfalls.
Emerald streams invade the riverbeds.
Spring pathways parade before the Summer show.
Big Horn and Elk graze with indifference.
Black Bears and Grizzlies begin to appear.
Native lore markers proclaim belonging.
Newcomer names hail early explorers.
Remnants of conquest and adventure speak.
Reminders of time's tale, traders and trains.
Salutes to survival and man-made feats.
Pursue the balance of the new and old.
Rim the Kicking Horse rails on to Kamloops,
vowing to return to Canada's wild.

Winter's Advent

Welcome to Canada's early winter
where the Fall showcase of nature's brilliance
is cut short by a sudden burst of white
blowing north from Lawrence's chilling yawn.
Thank you Gabriel for the safe passage
and silent steerage from your love angel
to the weekend warmth of Hovey Manor.
Heaven's wet white brushed the homeland slightly,
crimping the joy of Indian Summer,
while dressing the landscape for tomorrow
and setting La Table for communion.
Exquisite meal, exceptional exchange,
tapping the delight of the Loire Valley,
savoring Hatley's spectacular cuisine,
tossing tales embellished with uneven truths,
the sum of which fades with winter's greeting,
leaving the bounty of friendship in place
to last beyond the maple leaf's season.

Grand Canyon Rim

Behold the grandeur of canyon contours
exposing a slice of Nature's still life
marked by time on the Great Southwest Plateau,
set indifferent to time and circumstance.

Panchromatic hues from umber to beige
splashed with purple and red fossil fingers
etched in sandstone scars and graced in silence,
stare outwardly in shades of light and dark.

Geological lines testifying
to tales of spent ages without witness,
showcasing the bosom of Mother Earth,
exposing sacred grounds of ancient worlds.

Outer space turned inward in stoic stance
displaying the Unfathomable Pit
heightening curiosity and awe,
humbling human prowess and certainty.

Walk the rim of the giant panorama,
treading the crushed pebbled paths carefully
noticing ragged walls touch the skyline,
wondering what is on the other side.

(Courtesy of Robert Olson)

Tahoe Blue

Tahoe blue turns to indigo at night,
blinking stellar lights lace a cobalt sky
hovering over the Sierra woods,
beaming silence on unsuspecting souls
until dawn returns to reset the clock.

Meanwhile Tahoe stillness shadows daylight,
clouding our search for meaning and beyond
prompting science to explain ties to the void,
shaking confidence with uneasy doubt
to dismiss time until we disappear.

But life and loss teach us about living,
telling us to touch the beauty we see
and share one's love with friends and family,
letting the brightness restore faith to somewhere,
hoping the universe is unending.

Interlude

Time out! Dream on! Before continuing, though, let's take a musical respite and enjoy the instrumental interlude "Can't Stop" from the music selections. We then can move from sepia musings and Wordscapes to Voices Within humming word music and whispering images and insights on some gnawing questions about life, while keeping a smile.

Endless Beginnings

We know beginnings start in the middle,
nesting somewhere between before and after,
witnessing what we profess to be new.

Feel the fabric of the sky blue cover,
wearing white puffs or sometimes streaks of gray,
waiting for the night and dawn to return.

Celebrate the recurring beginnings,
making time ageless and age meaningless,
remembering times passed and promises to keep.

Share this treasure with family and friends,
basking in the warmth of relationships,
knowing new beginnings start all the time.

As I was saying ...

What does it all mean when our days are gone?
Remember playing games and having fun,
enjoying moments with no tomorrow,
celebrating occasions as they come.

Time is a stealth dagger that creeps along.
It lets us believe in roads without end,
teasing our minds with beauty and power,
getting in the way of chasing our dreams.

What does it all mean when there are no answers?
Daunting doubt defies our sense of being,
clouding hopes of confidence while awake,
chasing memories of lost ones until gone.

Obsession with work steals from life's bounty
Routine stifles imagination and defers dreams,
compromising the promise of each day,
losing sight of freedom's fantasy.

As I was saying, "I think that I know."
Life is about love, hope, uncertainty,
being aware of time as the arbiter,
living our dreams with every day we own

Part 2, Voices Within

Hear voices within whisper honesty,
expressing thanks and searching for meaning,
private stirrings of a curious mind,
stretching possibilities to the end.

Inner Spaces and Reflections in Blue Notes

Mind and heart define us. We see through the mind's eye and feel through the heart's beat. They are the soulful means that allow us to contemplate our existence and extend our sense of being. Waves of thought let us see clearly and create an assortment of meaning from fragments of experience. Our body rhythm absorbs the sound of music. The spirit tempers contradictions and adds value to life.

Peer into my morning mirror where another me spontaneously mimics a fool behind the face in the glass and an inner self solemnly peeks back. See how fun and doubt converge momentarily inside a complex persona. Join me in stealing time and putting jest aside to contemplate the awe of the world and our reason for being. Take a Dream Ride and slide down the dark hole of night chasing trapped thoughts and floating emotions. Listen to voices within whisper lyrics of love and old refrains, harmonize reflections in blue notes and rephrase "living tomorrow today" against the backdrop of the new realities after 9/11. Feel the retracing of my steps and a *Rhythm and Muse* sign off with sentimental End Notes.

Whisper

Lyrics by Sylvia MacCalla (CD)

We sometimes get in a rut in life
Nothing changes much from day to day
We wake up to the same face in the same place
The grass is always greener so they say
I never seem to know what's on your mind.
I never seem to find the time
I can barely hear my laughter through the pain.
Oh Lord I think I'm going insane.

But then I hear you whisper and it was
All I could hear nothing but your whisper
It made everything clear that all I want,
and all that I need is right here with me.

Livin' in a world of ups and downs
you were always there for me.
Through the times you never once complained.
No you gave it all
I've just forgotten why I didn't fall.
I never seem to know what's on your mind
I never seem to find the time
I can barely hear my laughter through the pain.
Oh Lord I think I'm going insane.

But then I hear you whisper and it was clear
All I could hear nothing but your whisper
It made everything clear that all I want,
and all that I need is right here with me.

Your love brought me in from the rain
I guess I've forgotten how to smile
then right beside me there you stood and
you've been standing there all the while.

Dream Ride

Dreams are mind twists of dormant desires,
a wishful sleep walk in a safe haven,
tethered to the comfort of inner space,
mixing the real with possibilities.

Crawl into the awaiting night capsule.
Escape the routine that triggers the launch.
Probe for lost episodes to play again.
Relish the fanciful with unmatched skills.
Build adventure with fragments from real-time.
Dodge death daily in persistent battles.
Fly over tall trees and ocean patches.
Invite imagination without guilt.
Release the power of uncanny charm.
Treasure the silent excitement alone.

Enjoy forever on the cushioned ride,
until you sense the sound of re-entry
shaking you alive to greet a new day,
erasing incoherence from the files.

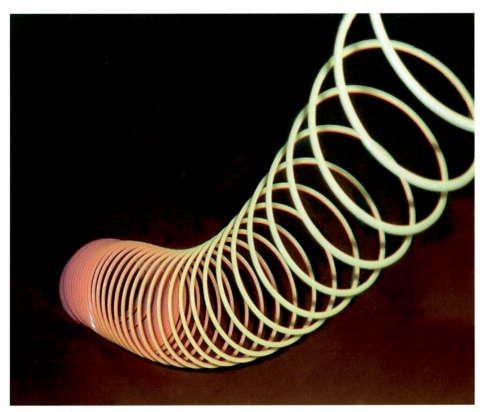

"Slinky" Courtesy of Evan Masterman

About Time

Time is now, whenever, and forever,
relentless reminder of our limits,
a creeping shadow on an endless path,
indifferent arbiter of choices,
declaring ownership temporary.

Time is the stealth tracker of joy and loss,
silent story-teller without a plot
perennial prowler in plural worlds,
telling believers and doubters the truth.

Time frames our existence and memory,
a phantom watcher of endless ages,
measuring the length of the journey home,
tempering our thoughts of life without end.

Faith on the Line

Why does doubt haunt the now and forever?

Our faith is undressed by time,
torn by inherited fear,
preying on curious minds,
pitting known against unknown,
breeding new contradictions,
stripping layers from taught truths
purging fragile certitude,
veiled by grace and hope,
waiting for salvation's sign.

Can a passion for Love cure the ailment?

Old Refrain

As we know, all beginnings start in the middle,
some with remembered before and wishful after

Roam within the hollow dark of self and listen
to parading sounds of wonderment and hope.

Balance the deep blue notes with contrasting colors
that give perspective to human error and sadness.

Why do we rush to the unwelcome finish line
when we still have time to spend and places to go?

Think about turning work into endless play,
while basking in the sun of curiosity.

Be thankful for wakeful moments and happy within,
living your dreams and plowing tomorrow's promise.

Wonderment

Each of us contemplates our existence alone.

We live in wonderment
asking fearful questions
getting doubtful answers
without resolution.

Each of us fears the unknown housed within us.

We ignore life's essence,
struggling to hide from death,
questioning assurance
to free ourselves from fate.

Each of us lives interdependently together

We grapple with knowing,
curious about truth,
searching the soul with hope
to discover the self.

Do we struggle to survive, evolve or transcend?

Blasphemy

We are a fascinating machine,
fiber wired with complex controls,
programmed to search an endless unknown.
We run on ignorance and choices,
tripped by doubt, haunted by fear of pain,
mesmerized by hope and lasting love.
We are born and meant to multiply
captive by self- imposed commitments
to family and a Great Unknown Force.
We want to revel in fantasy,
create a personal history,
propel ourselves into forever.

What if we are only machine-like,
lured into a sense of uniqueness,
led through an infinite labyrinth.
What if we challenge the Holy Words
mixing belief and doubt with hope,
until we are engulfed by the void.
What if we believe our innocence,
follow the lure of the after-life,.
gamble the present for future gains.
What if we deplete nature's treasures,
allow greed to devalue their worth,
deprive generations of their lot.

How long can living memories last?
Do lost loves swim in dreams, drown in sleep?
Will tomorrow disappear in space?

Reality

Whether or not you heed the warning signs
the road dead ends in a matter of time.

Catch the spirit of another day's song.
Embrace the sounds and enjoy the moment.
Hear time creeping in the swirling silence.
Drown the beat with shared love and fantasy.
Now listen to aging hearts grow carefree,
pacing the inevitable surrender
and getting ready to leave tomorrow.

Whether or not you follow the footsteps,
the time remaining is all that you have.

Hope

Coming together is about becoming community,
searching for meaning and sharing our pride.

Believing in tomorrow is about investing in dreams,
seeking wisdom to redefine the past.

Praying in Babylon breeds convictions rewoven in chaos,
growing hordes of newcomers to choose sides.

Clinging to yesterday compromises possibilities,
crimping the power of pluralism.

Savor the belief in a supreme light piercing the darkness,
knowing honest hope slays uncertainty.

Are you there somewhere?

Where are all those people who are roaming in my head,
kept alive by memories that soon will fade away?

Why is my mind so anxious and eager to feed doubt,
wanting to believe beyond, but falling prey to now?

How can we believe in the promise of tomorrow
when inhumanity contradicts our faith and hope?

Where are you loved ones?

They existed once, living life, leaving memories.
We save our past, remembering good, soothing sorrow.

They bridge the unknown with the promise of lasting peace.
We pursue dreams, make choices, and pray to live again.

They disappear into the mystery of darkness.
We, too, will join those legions who may have transformed from dust.

Are you there somewhere?

In Between

Life without love and no belief in beyond is meaningless.
Death is the permanent dot on life's finite continuum,
a constant reminder of the free gift of daily living
and silent passage to the deep caverns of infinity.

Life lets us enjoy the warmth of wholeness and family love.
Death is a port of call on the open sea, not journey's end,
a solitary respite on the way to eternity
and a reserve ticket to the greatest show in the universe.

Hopefully, we can enjoy the precious moments in between.

Limbo

Limbo is an unknown place in time,
a sanctuary for repentance,
wishful way station of the faithful
billed as a respite for forgiveness.

Limbo is suspended forever,
a mindless space reserved for doubters,
battling the phantom of survival,
questioning life, searching for answers

Limbo is a refuge with promise,
a vast wasteland between dusk and dawn,
imaginary darkness that stalks
until the chance of rescue appears.

Limbo is tomorrow's vestibule,
a half-way house for anointed souls,
and nowhere land to countless billions
wrapped in rituals on different shores.

Knowing More

I don't know you and you don't know me.
We speak to ourselves in silent tongues.
We breathe ballads from voices within.
We share life with our singular souls

You don't know you and I don't know me.
Our probe of self is mysterious.
Our songs to each other reveal most.
Our sharing of life is incomplete.

We know each other to a limit.
We try to love each other fully.
We shed life and cross the line alone.
I'll know you and you'll know me, then.

While We're Alive

Death touches each of us differently,
speaking to everyone through memories,
seeding the hope of a new beginning
or insisting it is the final act.

Life is created as a proving ground,
compromised by change and contradiction,
filled with intrigue, despair, sorrow and joy
armed with love and faith to win the grand prize.

We know what we know and feel confident,
despite the gnawing of humility,
telling us that knowledge is not wisdom
and understanding fully makes us whole.

Wonderment opens minds and tests beliefs.
letting us chase dreams and search for meaning,
weighing options of doubt and conviction,
caring for each other while we're alive.

Word Music

Words are the music of the mind and heart,
scoring ideas, circling emotions,
phrasing memories and conversations,
playing imagination's silent songs
with narrative notes and voices in verse
that allow us to let the inside out
and float between discord and harmony,
echoing sounds of a curious self,
freeing the spirit to search for meaning,
while telling something about who we are.

(Courtesy of Marcus Emerson)

Free Fall

Can we set our imagination free
to create mental pictures in color
and flirt with images that tease the mind?

Suppose we saw sameness in difference,
contrasting iron rails with rows of tulips
to invite wanderlust and showcase Spring.

Can we envision a timeless journey
that explores fields of curiosity
while leading and learning in the open?

Why not compose make-believe in real time,
inviting innocence to ride somewhere
to enjoy the grandeur of simplicity.

Let's play with wisdom's whims in offbeat chords
without tradition getting in the way
and hear voices within touch tomorrow.

Silent Song

Instantly, tomorrow is yesterday,
reminding us today is time we own
to fly away and chase our fantasies.

Imagination bridges the unseen,
allowing us to fathom forever
and override contradictions with faith.

As we continue to search for meaning
pause and think about how we came to be,
knowing today will never be the same.

Enjoy the warmth of being loved and free,
remembering yesterday, living now,
dreaming of tomorrows that may not come.

Praise the innocence in eyes of children,
aware of how time will steal it away
and let them discover truth on their own.

Create a special place with openness
where we are true to ourselves and others,
and our belief systems find common ground.

Nature's Backyard

She painted the forest sentinels white,
accenting winter's carpet with tips of
vibrant green branches peeking through the frost,
guarding the wonderland at equinox,
silently portraying simple beauty.

He asked her to stay awhile and breathe life
while waiting for admirers to come
and appreciate the Master's art work
rendered on an alabaster canvas,
inviting all to share the open backyard

(Courtesy of Glynn Masterman)

Rooftops

Rooftops dot shrub-laden hillsides at dawn,
overlooking earth's watery domain,
in the company of a man and his dog.

Vista vanguards symmetrically aligned,
anchored from sunrise to sunset's parade,
dressing drab contours for morning strollers.

Ridgeline sentinels staring to the west
indifferent to the surf's crashing sound,
yielding to the blue expanse of Nature.

Stand steadfast and lifeless on borrowed land
while your shelter presence is overlooked
until time and nature reclaim the soil.

Morning Stroller

Some mornings the sky is clear, placid blue.
Other days it stares with hanging soot clouds.
Today it greets me with cheerful brilliance.
I can't wait to see what tomorrow brings.

Walks with Alex

Do dogs see rooftops or the ocean's edge touch the sky?
Do dogs have the same wonder of mind we claim to own?

Come with me on a dog walk to greet the morning sun,
stopping every now and then to breathe grateful sighs,
listening to birds sing and chat to accent the silence
and gracefully welcome the dawning of a new day.

Alex leads and follows depending upon his mood,
meandering with alertness and indifference,
letting you know in his simple way that he's aware
of the surroundings and quiet threats, despite dumbness.

Wandering walks reveal subtle treasures of stillness,
allowing us to peek through Nature's mirror
and question why only we can know and animals
are beings with instincts and lost souls without free will.

Let's take this dirt path up the hill that may lead nowhere,
guessing on what lies ahead without seeking answers,
or responding to cues from our loyal companion
who's ready to continue in any direction.

Let's turn around and head back to familiar ground,
believing in ourselves and the virtue of openness
to thwart ignorance and the fallacy of blind faith,
lest we mar a memorable dog walk etched in time.

Anywhere Bridge

I offered her unencumbered love to learn more about life.
Maybe she'll return my love and I'll live long enough to know.

Once upon the Anywhere Bridge I fell in love with the world.
It was dawn rising with first signs of light on the horizon,
beckoning everyone on this side of the earth to see.
She smiled at me in stillness, dressed in wavy Blue Pacific,
disguising her watery might with an overwhelming smile.

In an instant, I knew how fortunate I was to meet her,
so I released my heart to chase the mystery beyond the edge.
Outfitted with curiosity and imagination
I was confident that the journey would yield hidden treasures,
with insights on the persistence of love and hate around us .

Aware of the time-and-place phenomenon of happenings
I knew that there were suitors seeing her through other windows.
The Gray Atlantic's water face wears a different mood,
displaying her bold beauty with unpredictable movement,
while other folks on other shores lay claim to water wonders.

Instantly everyone can fathom how fortunate they are,
but often withhold wishes and judgments their heart and mind make.
Not dismayed by the fraction of the globe that land occupies,
people continue to bully and march foolishly as giants
unaware of how far the line is drawn in a finite world.

With a heart set free and a probing mind I danced the dawn away.
It is a rare moment that one can see the world through the cracks
and experience insightful flashes reflected in the ocean.
She turns into a spiritual love freeing me from the cage,
raising soulful questions that only peace with oneself allows.

Why do some live in yesterday and believe in forever,
while others live in now and believe tomorrow man can make?
Contrast the crashing of waves with its spent surf washing ashore,
humbling us with its great expanse and a gentle reminder
to forgive, enjoy life fully with care, and shape a future.

Her luring beauty speaks many tongues courting would-be callers.
I thought I heard her say my name, but that was me wanting more.

Seeing the world through the cracks

Within Earth's walls we can see ourselves inverted,
staring at unevenness in everyday life
unable to interpret the signs overhead.

Consider the unknown and the unknowable
and try seeing an endless universe through the cracks
that reveal the nakedness of cherished beliefs.

Reflect on the assumptions of natural order
and professions of faith that testify to truth
to span the cruel chasms of despair and hope.

Notice a fragmented world arguing nonsense
building sandcastles of fortune to conquer fear
and disguise hollowness while searching for meaning.

Listen to varied voices of people and thought
seeking unity amidst the clash of cultures
so we can understand and live in harmony.

Within these walls we can find answers and solace,
envisioning possibilities without fault
and knowing that love and forgiveness will prevail.

Life's Work

Have you ever thought of time taking its toll before your eyes,
wondering whether old art and craft's tradition will survive?
Generational skills of old trades have been buried by change,
popular culture, and the pressures of globalization.
Goods and service now reflect timely transworld parts assembly
and Kentucky blue grasslands welcome foreign auto makers.

What happened to the legacies of artisans and craftsmen,
master men of the grandfather clocks and the banjo maker?
Gone are barbers who cut children's hair at home on Saturday,
those who fixed things, painted rooms, made slipcovers, and clothes on call.
We have witnessed the fading of novel hand-made creations
and stilting labor, whisked abroad in a new economy.

What if we journeyed to the Heartland, the South, or New England
looking for vestiges of yesterday's skills practiced today?
Traverse the Beautiful from the Northwest to Florida's Keys
to revitalize community as keeper of life's work.
Find telling stories, sing the praise, and celebrate mastering
to generate a critical force for preserving lost art.

Living Tomorrow Today

Yesterday at 9/11

Spurred by the love and lure of daily life, I put the notion of "We" to music and started sorting the enigmas. Then, Yesterday at 9/11, the hurtful spike of terror struck and changed the world we thought we knew. Instantly, our vulnerability on the planet was magnified and our sense of interdependence was shaken. The aftermath not only prompted national reflection, but also a resolve that stirred a new togetherness. The pain moved us to reassess everyday assumptions, remembering that man's nature is basically good. It encouraged me to sing life aloud with kin to express appreciation for simple truths and what really matters. I invite you to listen and hear a fellow person put humanness into perspective.

We as One

We is a wonderful word that
symbolizes the love in us,
bonding men, women, and children
rolled into a wide world of hope,
seeking love, joy, and openness,
knowing some do not understand
out of ignorance and despair.

We is a beautiful word that
explains shared purpose in life,
attuned to human frailty
with inherent contradictions,
prone to anger and foolishness,
harboring hate, rage and revenge
yet able to forgive and heal.

We is a powerful word that
unites us in times of crisis,
battling the ills that divide us
and forces that violate us,
pursuing a passion for peace
to preserve freedom and justice
and save the soul of We as One.

War with Peace

War is an act of human behavior,
flawed display of power and ignorance
that mesmerizes free will and destroys
natural states for greed and honor's sake.

War is a game that is played out of fear,
set in innocence, unleashed in madness
to rationalize ideologies
so that the rule of law or might survive.

Peace is the desire of humankind,
universal lure for world harmony
mobilizing the spirit against war
to heal the ravage of insanity.

Peace is the silent prayer of many tongues
offered alone or en masse on the streets
to counter senseless carnage and distrust
and borrow time to forgive and forget.

Tomorrow's Tapestry

Feel the new millennium tapestry - -
Democracy defines diversity
Equality is mutual respect
Citizenship creates whole community
Freedom frames and fuels the human spirit.
Caring is a global imperative.
Identity is a personal choice
World-views reflect the challenges of change.
Spirituality breeds faith and hope
Science questions and approximates truth
A child is the world's legacy of love.

9/11 after Five

Five years ago on September 11, 2001, *"We as One"* was written as a response to what was a day of disbelief. A blatant rage of terror struck two Manhattan pillars that symbolized economic global dominance and indifference in a divided world. In an instant, tragedy was replaced with widespread sorrow and a united front against such insanity. What started out as a concerted reaction against the specter of terrorism became a convoluted war of wills and personal questioning of being, belonging, and the future of civility and humankind.

It seems appropriate to remember that senseless day with a sequel verse that changes the focus from macro tragedy to micro reality. We can learn a lot from that clash of despair and righteousness. Hopefully, the best of our human spirit will prevail to let us grow a more equitable interdependent world community and caring global civil society.

Why and For What

We are ruled by the fear of the unknown,
question our being and purpose in life,
and live with faith and hope to keep us whole.

We are bred to believe and procreate,
preserve the lines that ensure tomorrow,
despite distrust and reigns of ignorance.

Logic leads to the inevitable,
and discoveries shatter firm beliefs
that turn faith and fear into a holy war.

Accept the twists in man-made rules
with the limitations they represent
and learn to live with change as a constant.

Love life, respect human differences
to counter hate and wrath of violence
and foster the power of shared knowledge.

Embrace togetherness as a pathway
for survival and global peace of mind,
since we all want to know why and for what.

TAM
9/11/06

(Courtesy of Reuben MacCalla)

New Day's Hope

Say hello to another day's human drama,
cast by daily records of orderly chaos,
scripted by Nature, daring, and the commonplace,
performed by restless players from heaven and hell,
costumed in cultural habits and varied tongues,
suspicious of constant change that caters to need.

As we hail the lure of peace and prosperity,
see how we cling to those lessons that lord our lives,
reveling in the joy of life to hide suffering,
singing the lyrics of love to overcome hate,
hoping that this year's dawning will brighten tomorrow,
granting wishes while we circle the sun again.

Pursue this new beginning with optimism,
renewing the promise of possibilities,
while amplifying freedom's resonating sound,
amidst distrust, rage, and turmoil among brethren,
reaffirming faith in the human family
so that prayers of love and forgiveness will be heard.

What would you do if you could change the world?

Energy is the secret source of life
hidden in science and mysteries of faith
buried in the bowels of the universe.
How can we unlock the critical codes
and record the logic of the known
to create waves of change and add value?

Why yield to tradition without question
adhering to wishful wisdom and fear.
Curious minds challenge the assumptions,
reordering the logic of the known
to find ways to exploit ideas for good
and create opportunities for growth.

What would you do if you could change the world?
Some people build great castles in the sky.
Others fly away because they know how,
sharing knowledge to make a difference,
and exploring the possible on earth
fusing ions for the good of mankind,

You can change the world through discovery,
knowing more about how energy works,
coupling faith with fact to fill the gaps,
cultivating intimacy with self
to find mindfulness and listening beyond
for signals blocked by our conditioning.

Burning Questions

Seeking unity with diversity
sounds like a never ending melody
that only the privileged few can hear.

By believing that we are at the threshold
of a brave new world clashing with the old
lets us reflect on possible futures.

Can hope and caring survive the fires
of hatred, distrust, greed, and righteousness
that can destroy our universal bond?

Twisted minds shaped by fanaticism
seek to rule the globe with fear and terror
to create a new world order of pain.

Creative minds wrought from curiosity
seek to discover new ways of thinking
that offer pathways to share tomorrow.

How can we reconcile these divergent poles
amidst distorted truth for hidden gains
that crimps desires of democracy.

War and violence are the enemies
as is indifference to human needs
or the shroud of ignorance and despair.

Peace and forgiveness are counter forces
as is freedom and mutual respect
or sustaining the quality of life.

What can we do together to live as one?
Who knows and Who cares? Who can and Who will?
These are the burning questions of our time.

What If

Curiosity and humor abound,
freedom releases imagination,
allowing knowledge to grow and be shared.

Everyone has a story to tell,
a song to sing or fantasy on hold,
searching for listeners and open minds.

What if trust was the order of the day,
compromise and kindness the rule of law
and the search for truth a private matter.

What if we could live tomorrow today
and play with ideas as a given right
to shape the future for the good of all.

What if we could follow intuition
and create a caring, prosperous world
that thrives on respect and human concern.

What if everyone could wear a smile
and don the spirit of discovery
in search of countless possibilities.

Opportunity

Opportunity surrounds open minds,
awaiting the call of daring dreamers
who want to toy with old and new ideas
and run the course of possibilities.

Opportunity breeds lasting life skills
for personal rewards and common good,
shaping the spirit of entrepreneurs,
leading, growing, and creating value.

Live in the house opportunity built
with innovation, trust and good fortune,
coupled with time, talent and integrity
to be shared with those willing to invest.

Schooling Alone

Power, privilege, and faith rule the world,
order and chaos shape the universe.

We are taught to seek wisdom and obey,
live and let live, love, believe and be free.

Why should we have to wait for tomorrow
when everyone's ready to play today?

Beliefs are customs privately reframed,
giving meaning to life and hope's logic.

Times change much faster than the people do,
fueling resistance to shifting values.

Why not risk the private thoughts that guide us,
even though the questions may be disturbing?

Problems seeking solutions are endless,
so we do what we can, grin and bear it.

Why can't we learn to fly away alone,
dream aloud, invest in life-long learning?

Reality Shows

Chasing fulfillment in the raw has popular appeal,
promoting the whims of winning against the odds,
pitting independence against fleeting relationships,
contesting wit, skill, and values in veiled environments
to praise perseverance as the true measure of success.

Another reality show has a different script,
seeking attention and relief amidst indifference,
searching for survival and self-reliance with no voice,
hoping the pursuit of innovation and compassion
wins the prize of human worth and mutual respect.

Culture is compromised in the new knowledge sharing show,
shattering an old world with delicate discoveries,
exposing tradition's assumptions, customs, and beliefs,
making reflection and compromise emerging standards
for bridging deep differences and finding common ground.

Episodes recognize chaos and the constant of change,
breeding cyber citizens at risk in uncertainty,
protesting the waste of privilege and plight of the poor,
confronting tyranny and the politics of power
to champion equality, social justice and world peace.

Tied to purpose and passion, perseverance is success,
leading change to improve the quality of life for all,
running risks, seizing opportunities, adding value,
living fully with the consequences of our choices
so the free-fall context of reality is routine.

Tracing My Steps

Recall

Great moments in the early years of life
stir the embers of cherished memories
stretching the recall of personal feats,
buried in the thickets of fantasy,
shining shadows and guiding heroics
to package personal glory for fun.

From the unbelievable Prep School catch
to the unreal blast to deep center field
From American Legion sandlot cheers
to the frightening sounds of the battlefield,
confidence grows to grip uncertainty
and make destiny's winter bearable.

Half-forgotten tales waiting to be retold
with persuasion and unchallenged details
are rephrased for believability,
along with remnants of private moments
disguised by twists in life's daily routine
but let us recall and rescue lost worlds.

Doubting Thomas

Sepia seed keep blossoming in Babylon,
maturing in search of the message of meaning,
awaiting tomorrow's perpetual promise
amidst a world espousing competing unknowns.

Life continues fooling fools caught in forever,
shrinking cherished circles with sunrise and sunsets,
stretching moments to disguise our fears with prayer,
muting salvation's call with temporal pleasures

We assume time will last and squander its treasure.
We also sense the sand filling the glass bottom.
Value life and purse its meaning with passion,
even though uncertainty plagues our destiny.

We know what we know and believe with confidence.
We also know that we don't know much and live lies.
Value the knowing and the innocence of truth,
replacing the wisdom of fools with new knowledge.

Hopefully an All-Knowing Power will appear,
revealing the infinite beauty of beyond,
forgiving honest doubters wanting to believe,
preserving faith and free will in a finite world.

Invisible Me

I've been called "boy" when I was a man,
obeyed the rules and snubbed righteousness.
I've been a soldier in wasted wars,
battled closed minds, crossed the color line.
But you should know there are two of me,
peaceful persuader and warrior,
yearning to tell the tale of blackness
with the freedom of being oneself,
blending history's reminders with
tomorrow's voice of imagination.

Black Star, always trying to prove things,
ready to defy low expectations,
accepting success with second place.
Black Sage, ancient son of survival,
knowing when to shout and be silent,
touching hard hearts with soulful truths.
Behold the power of the white moon
overshadowing the stellar lights
that blur the dots of the milky way,
until we can free ourselves to see.

Time reveals the depth of ebony,
creative, though dismissed or excused,
with some respect given in private.
Beneath honest smiles is a person,
blessed with pride and a family crown,
warring to overcome the twoness.
Live with the invisible mirror,
seizing the earned power of knowledge
so new dark stars can shine in the night
and bury the hurt of ignorance.

Nothing New

Why fret over being invisible?

No one can build or own a dream alone,
whether shaped in words, deeds, or images,
our passions reflect shares in a vision
created somewhere with others in time.

We scour fields of compassionate ore,
seeking like minds to embellish the quest,
laying bare our secrets with openness
to seek trust and forge an open exchange.

We toil to showcase our wishful wonder,
aware of poachers in the marketplace,
risk is reduced to false sense of pride,
enduring hurt as the price of the prize.

No one can boast or claim single success,
though honestly gained or widely perceived
New is an uncanny twist of the Old,
changing course for universal knowledge.

Salty Snippet, Prelude to "Little Switch"

Marines like telling tall tales, but they know that the "little ones" tend to stick and beg an audience. Let me share a salty snippet that I recounted to my sons. I told them about two familiar Marine Corps refrains: "Hurry up and wait" and "Move out" and that the first was a taste of discipline and the second a test of will. Even though Marines are supposed to tackle the near-impossible unflinchingly, I let them know that the ghost of the unpredictable tends to haunt the halls. When "Move Out" is issued, the duty signal has a way of driving a person beyond normal limits.

Such was a string of lost days in March of '53 when a lull in the "Korean Conflict" went haywire. In December, 1952, our home away from home was characterized by drab clumps of mountain peaks called the "Nevada cities" - - Vegas, Carson, Reno, Boulder, and later Elko. These desert citadels were the hills that housed strategic battle positions that were to be defended as one's castle. Fortunately, for me, the place was built and paid for before I arrived. Nonetheless, the mortgage was not guaranteed. All I had to do was to hurry up and get acquainted with the surroundings so that I could learn how to live with the unpredictability of war. These Nevada cities protected the gateway to Seoul. They were vital landmarks to the rear commanders, but to the junior officers and their men they were dirt piles with holes to dig. The automatic response was to be a grunt and carry on.

Maps are maps. They mark spots and chart distances. Central Korea west of Seoul was no different. On our map, the battlefield was a cordoned-off, sliver of land labeled Panmunjon. It was a deceptive piece of earth that haunted the night and unnerved the day with contentious war and peace talks and stalemate sessions. Deadly enemies were separated outside the tented walls by a buffer zone called "no-man's land," reminding each side of their nearness. The artificial turf was routinely punctuated with eerie surveillance noise, night patrols, and propaganda taunts. My 81 mortar platoon was somewhat distanced from the area of intrigue, but very much in touch with its vulnerability, which became very clear when I later was assigned to the demilitarized zone's Out Post #2. This lull in the hot and cold "police action" was beginning to wane as a dreadful March madness was gearing up to roar.

It didn't take long to learn about the unevenness of troop strength and effectiveness of equipment. Not all platoons had three mortar support squads with ample tubes, base plates, and ammo at the ready. When hell surfaced and the Chinese and North Koreans decided to move the political pawns for table-talk leverage, we restarted the night game. The military masterminds knew how to counter and ordered the "men in the field" to standby and be ready to move out on a moment's notice. That decision translated into counter-attack on demand because faceless hordes periodically attempted to overrun UN positions.

In a desperate move, I was ordered to leave my rear mortar-haven and lead a make-shift "rescue and reinforcement" team to a forward position that was under fire and in desperate need of help. Marine psychology kicked in. Numbness took over and the invincible serum began to take hold. The thrown-together battle crew was less-than platoon strength, forcefully cast as a dutiful family on a mission. The "hurry-up" had no waiting time and the "move out" shout was short and a little incomprehensible. With instilled confidence, this ad hoc contingent was set to follow their young second-lieutenant's commands without hesitation. Very shortly, the search orders became educated guesses wrapped in faith and intuition.

Although we stayed intact, carrying our gear and fear into the unknown, communications became a problem. At the outset, my "sugar" calling code and radio signals to the rear were crisp and coherent. With each step forward, though, they would become increasingly blurred and problematic. Without warning, a cryptic call crowded the lines and I found myself on the receiving end of conversation with the enemy feigning as friend. I heard a wolf in sheep's clothing wrestling with vowels and consonants. The strange voice was soliciting a response to a "sugar tear to sugar zero" transmission, insisting on my position and asking me to keep talking. It didn't take much to know that we were in trouble and I remembered what mamma told me what to do when you hit bottom - be cool. Spared by darkness and calm, I let my voice deliver the confidence needed to stealthily withdraw. I shut down the radio talk and said quietly, "Keep moving, follow me."

Fortunately, the enemy was equally dismayed. When we reached our objective, we discovered a grim hilltop of worthless dirt littered with the fallen from both sides and cloaked in silence. We stared in awe, ready to respond   My next command was reflexive, "Let's get the hell out of here."

God led the way. No sooner had we cleared the mounds with break-neck speed, we headed back together with an inner sense of direction. Suddenly the sky screamed with rounds of friendly ordinance bursting on the hill we left behind. Obviously a strike was ordered without a request. We recovered our wits in an instant, and I often wondered whether those inaudible "sugar tear" signaling and repeated "come in" calls with the fumbling "r" sounds may have contributed to the artillery furry that said "obliterate." The thrill came when we realized that enough time had passed after our departure and allowed the enemy time to occupy the space we left. The fire storm found its mark and kept the other swarm of night killers at bay.

The trek back seemed fast, as though we took a short-cut so that we could return to our lines by intermission. All I can remember is thanking the conscripted stragglers from assorted companies, wishing them well, and jumping into a ditch at the sound of enemy "incoming." Shrapnel tapped my helmet and I relieved myself. The bombardment did not last long. It was like an enemy message responding angrily to their miscalculation. The dim of night was followed by air strikes. The Marines rained hell on all forward positions and eventually retook lost ground. The no-name rescue mission ended and the odd group returned to their unit or Casual Company. Undoubtedly, the tale would gather salt and be recounted in vivid colors somewhere, someday.

After a short stint as a platoon commander defending a rear post at the mouth of the ancient Korean burial grounds known as the "Valley of the Moon," I became the division historian. When the word came down that the peace talks had progressed and that a good-faith prisoner-of-war exchange would take place, I got a chance to write an innocuous piece of history and an anecdotal record in the Command Diary.

It started with Operation Little Switch, the first P.O.W. exchange before the war-ending "Operation Big Switch" in August. Fortunately, I was one of the first people on the scene. I decided to follow my curiosity and be the cub reporter with an angle. I spotted the first returnee a Marine P.O.W. and followed him through the exchange process from beginning to end.

That subject turned out to be a Lieutenant Colonel, the highest ranking Marine returnee. It also led to a very unusual telephone call weeks later in the relative comfort of the Rear. Evidently, the United Nations Command was tardy getting first-day coverage on the high profile exchange and used some of my material for the opening record. Then one day, out of the blue, General Mark Clark, the United Nations Commander placed a direct call to my division historian tent and relayed a personal "thanks" for prefacing the "Little Switch" story. Needless to say, when the UN General spoke to me over the telephone, I never jump to attention so fast and so high. I stood frozen to listen to his kind words and locked the terse praise in the vault of my head. The experienced gilded the hurried rescue attempt on the hill. I was ready to write some more.

Naked Journey

Last night, I listened to my body speak to me
and discovered another meaning of twoness.
Like DuBois' truth of two black souls living in one,
my naked journey exposed the clouds of conflict.
I heard a dream coming and had to shadow it.

I followed the labyrinth of the quiet night
as a solitary creature probing new depths,
witnessing the spiritual power of insight.
Though impossible to explain a fantasy,
I could do so in this phantom state of unreal.

Suspended in the cave, I began to observe.
The brain would issue an innocuous command,
such as raise the prune juice spoon to the lower lip,
only to be foiled by a nanosecond light
that saw the hand move as spoon and lip disappear.

Free-falling in my abyss with laser vision,
I pierced the paradox of the split inner self,
unraveling the mystery of imagination,
making whole the distortions of human travail,
seeing the struggles of the darker brother end.

Black Star

Silent Black Star shine your light on the past,
exposing the wrongs of a righteous world.
Cast your stealth shadow on hypocrisy,
allowing democracy to flourish.

Resist inequity and injustice,
tearing down hate that houses ignorance.
Dismiss the hurt felt from devalued deeds,
stripping the glory from hard earned success.

Know the folly of whitewashing blackness,
prolonging pain with smiles and misplaced trust.
Slay stereotypes by opening minds
countering self blame and the victim's role.

Bridge the chasm of chaotic order
and raise forgotten black stars from the ash.
Make our history whole with rightful heirs,
balancing foul justice with fresh fairness.

Black Star still believing in the promise,
beaming rays of forgiveness and healing.
Own Langston's America Becoming
to help make the Grand Experiment real.

Dark Hope reach out, start the fire next time,
pursuing dreams with purpose and passion.
Embrace unity with diversity,
respecting difference for the common good.

Langston's Plea

Langston's America Becoming
still haunts the new millennium
amidst dividing culture clashes
casting shadows on becoming whole.

Langston's America can Become
empowered to slay its ignorance
and extend the Grand Experiment
to render freedom's colorless call.

Listen to Langston's prophetic plea
in his refrain of one from many
challenging custom, comfort, and greed,
forcing America to Become.

Gordon's Gift

Photojournalism is an art form,
capturing the essence of the moment,
skillfully interpreting the implied,
with light, angles, and the unspoken word
to state reality without comment.

In an instant, "What is" becomes "What if,"
documenting with the camera's eye,
while reproducing telling emotions,
portraying and projecting life in the raw
translated as poetic expression.

Renaissance man witnessing the struggle,
whether Choice of Weapons or Learning Tree,
storyteller of blight and becoming,
celebrate aloud with your special gift
visually recording lest we forget.

Lessons Learned

We learn to know life by welcoming it,
valuing old and discovering new.
We learn about love by sharing ourselves,
nurturing family relations and friendships.
We learn the sum of difference is whole,
respecting beliefs in an unknown world.
We learn to arrest fear with faith and hope,
discovering truth and balancing doubt
We learn the beauty of simplicity –
live honestly, let live, and leave a trail.

End Notes

After years of flirting with abstract notions and toying with verse, my world fell into place. I was committed to live insatiable dreams and write poetry with prose tied to the rhythmic beat of the heart. I dusted off years of false starts and rededicated myself to explain my reason for being. Along the way, I discovered the essence of family love and saw its reflection in our children. They abound in talent and I aspired to be like them. I latched onto their spiritual sense and the inner drive of a musical gift. I played sibling songs in colorful whole notes and half tones with my instrument of words. The result is this collection of *Rhythm and Muse*, a composition inspired by my lifelong wife and best friend and punctuated with the original music and loving lyrics of our offspring.

Music Makers

Music echoes the sweet sap of the soul,
releasing artistry to live freely,
surprising the casual listener,
while serenading the serious ear.
Music captivates the human spirit,
mesmerizing all in poetic ways,
creating rhythms resembling the old,
breathing new life into forgotten tunes.
Hear the fresh blend of new school and old school,
mixing today's beat with yesterday's sound,
meshing mellow syncopated blue notes,
with soulful kin voices "livin' out loud"

Old School, New School

Reproducing yesterday's moods,
giving old rhythms a new beat,
blending instrumentals with voice
to celebrate musicianship
is the bridge of old school, new school.

Phrasing lyrics as poetry,
creating original sounds,
remixing the familiar
to cross over with subtlety
as the ballad of a new day.

Playing to the music inside,
accompanied by rainbow chords,
drowning chants of no tomorrow
to ignite the youthful spirit.
is the soul of a bright future.

Steve's Unending Night

What do you know about Steve?

Steve Allen left the mike on,
joining those who went before,
reminding us in waiting
about muted memories.

Music maker, funny man
silenced by life's laser blade,
leaving riffs and laughs behind
to remember upbeat sounds.

Keep smiling with flatted fifths,
replaying tunes in our head,
tapping to a dated beat
that lasts with age and returns.

Humor and hidden blue notes
sustain your jazz legacy,
reliving yesterday's scene
even though few know your name.

Let fun and artistry thrive,
changing moods with the seasons,
beckoning joy's warmth to stay
to distract us from the end.

Good Night Steve, Late Show Hipster.

Until Tomorrow

I accept my many sides of being,
still questioning the unfathomable.
I admire culture's varied chorus lines
while listening to the sounds of logic.
I wonder what lies in the universe,
hoping to dispel my lingering doubt.
I know the answers outdistance the mind,
and preface the limits of tomorrow.
I appreciate owning memories
and the promise of everlasting love.

(Courtesy of Glynn Masterman)

Passing Thought

Aging has a way of crystallizing our moods,
dismissing the fantasy runs of youthful years
as good times of the moment with no tomorrow.

We swim in innocence until struck by reason,
wanting everything without paying in full
and trying to outdistance the shadow of time.

Growing older is a natural inconvenience,
hampering good intentions and crimping desires,
forcing acceptance of the choices we have made.

We peak with time and wonder about what remains,
wanting to forgive, forget, and survive the past
while feeling the joy and pride of running a good race.

The gradual slide seems to go faster than the climb,
being conscious of what we have not seen or done
recognizing the beauty and value of health.

If you are blessed with children and a loving mate,
mellowing together is a timeless treasure
where families grow as friends and mature as one.

Smile awhile, share the passion of being alive,
dispelling the fear of possible nothingness
and start sharing the hope of an eternal beyond.

Why hide from truth or fear the inevitable,
wondering about the days after tomorrow
when you can live forever now by being you.

About TAM

My name is Thomas or TAM in print. I was born in Bridgeport, Connecticut during the Crash of '29 and only those who left before me know when I will leave. I was raised by a loving family, with four older siblings and Doc and Esther as parents and role models. I was educated by the Jesuits, groomed by the Marine Corps, and blessed with JC, my life's treasure in a growing marriage of over fifty years, and four talented and caring children.

Professionally, I was an elementary and high school teacher, a college professor, assistant school superintendent, senior university administrator, publisher and editor of a specialized newspaper, *The Minority Enterprise*, an entrepreneur, and a dreamer. Graduated from Fairfield College Preparatory School (1947), received a bachelor's degree (1951) and master's degrees (1954) from Fairfield University. Earned a doctorate in education and American literature from the University of California, Los Angeles (1964) and completed a post-doctoral program in urban planning from UCLA (1976).

I always have been curious and wanting to be better. From childhood I was steeped in writing, music, and sports, waiting for my turn at bat or on the court. I wrote poems for personal pleasure and professional articles to validate my role as an educator. Through *Rhythm and Muse*, I want to share over seventy five years of life's adventure and start a new season on an upbeat.

TAM

3/20/06

Companion CD
Poetry Readings and Music Selections from
Rhythm & Muse, *Shades of Thought in Cadence and Voices Within*

- Endless Beginnings
- Music of the Mind
- We as One
- Shades of Thought in Cadence:
  Somewhere I heard a writer
  paint a song

- Tahoe Blue
- Grand Canyon Rim
- Walks with Alex

- Color of Life at Home:
  Inside the little room that felt large
- Evans of the World

- Sepia Saga
- Invisible Me
- The Measure of Self

- Voices Within
- Dream Ride
- You and Me

- Music Makers
- Silent Song

- Rx
- Let's Grow Our Love
- Tribute to JC
- Passing Thought

Love Joy (Introduction)

Can't Stop (Instrumental)

Whisper

What About Us (Instrumental)

I've Got to Be Strong

Love Joy (Refrain)

I Wanted You to Know

Sunshine (Instrumental)

KIN PRODUCTIONS

www.kinproductions.com